HORRID HENRY'S World Records

Francesca Simon spent her childhood on the beach in California, and then went to Yale and Oxford Universities to study medieval history and literature. She now lives in London with her family. She has written over fifty books and won the Children's Book of the Year in 2008 at the Galaxy British Book Awards for *Horrid Henry and the Abominable Snowman*.

Tony Ross is one of Britain's best-known illustrators, with many picture books to his name as well as line drawings for many fiction titles. He lives in the Welsh borders.

There are many more **HORRID HENRY**
books available.

For a complete list look at the
back of the book or visit
www.horridhenry.co.uk
or
www.orionbooks.co.uk

Francesca Simon
Illustrated by Tony Ross

Orion
Children's Books

First published in Great Britain in 2013
by Orion Children's Books
a division of the Orion Publishing Group Ltd
Orion House
5 Upper Saint Martin's Lane
London WC2H 9EA
An Hachette UK Company

1 3 5 7 9 10 8 6 4 2

Text © Francesca Simon 2013
Illustrations © Tony Ross 2013

The moral right of Francesca Simon and Tony Ross to be identified as author and illustrator of this work has been asserted.

Records compiled by Sally Byford.

The Orion Publishing Group's policy is to use papers that are natural, renewable and recyclable products and made from wood grown in sustainable forests. The logging and manufacturing processes are expected to conform to the environmental regulations of the country of origin.

ISBN 978 1 4440 0921 7

A catalogue record for this book is available from the British Library.

Printed in Great Britain by
Clays Ltd, St Ives plc

www.orionbooks.co.uk
www.horridhenry.co.uk

CONTENTS

Hello from Henry

World records? Bah! These are true world records. Top secret world records. The best world records, because most of them are all about ... ME! The World Record Champion of the Universe! Oh, and I should warn you, Peter has a few world records himself, but believe me, these are NOT world records anyone would ever want to win.

So read on . . . and marvel!

Henry

1. SPEED AND SKILL

WORLD'S FASTEST MAN

The fastest man in the world, even faster than Aerobic Al, is Usain Bolt from Jamaica, who holds the world record time of 9.58 seconds in the hundred-metre sprint.

AEROBIC AL
The world's fastest boy is ... grr ... Aerobic Al. But I did beat him once. Ha! Which makes ME the true world's fastest boy.

GREATEST GOALS
Footballer Pelé of Brazil has scored the most goals of any player during his football career – 1,279 goals in 1,363 games from 1956 to 1977. His best year was 1959 with an amazing 126 goals!

CAPTAIN OF THE FOOTBALL TEAM

Moody Margaret is the Captain of the Football Team and - unfortunately - the best footballer in my class. It's so unfair. She also holds the record for being the second best footballer in the class **AND** the third best footballer in the class. Rats.

SPEEDY PING-PONG

Jackie Bellinger and Lisa Lomas set a table tennis world record in 1993 by hitting 173 balls backwards and forwards in the space of a minute.

SPINNING TOPS

Magician Steve Faulkner from the UK set a spinning tops records in 2010 by spinning 22 tops all at the same time, using just one hand.

TOP SHOT

That's ME! I practised so hard with my Goo-Shooter that I once hit Peter's nose at thirty paces.

FINGER FOOTBALL CHAMPION

Raphael Harris of Israel holds the record for spinning a football on one finger – he can spin it for an incredible 4.21 minutes.

BEST BACKWARDS
In 2008, Kerstin Mennenga-Metzler
from Liechtenstein ran the Rome Marathon
in 4 hours 42 minutes and 39 seconds. That's
the fastest time someone has ever run a
marathon **BACKWARDS**!

MOST CUNNING CROSS-COUNTRY RUNNER

Me, obviously. Just listen to this cunning plan. I won the cross-country race at Sports Day by dropping sweets on the ground so the other runners stopped to pick them up. Then I sped past them all – even Aerobic Al – to be first across the finishing line! Genius.

CLEVER KICK-UPS
In 1995, Nikolai Kutsenko from the Ukraine juggled a football with his feet, legs and head for 24 hours and 30 minutes without the ball ever touching the ground.

LONGEST OCEAN SWIM

The furthest distance swum in the open sea without flippers is 225 kilometres by a Croatian called Veljko Rogosic. In 2006, he swam across the Adriatic Sea in 50 hours 10 minutes.

Naturally I could do that, but I'm too busy right now.

2. SUPER-SIZED

BEEFIEST BIG Z
Zydrunas Savickas, nicknamed "Big Z", is the World's Strongest Man. He's nearly two metres tall, weighs 175 kilogrammes and can lift a log weighing 220 kilogrammes – even heavier than himself!

Greedy Graham is copying him already.

BEEFY BERT

The biggest boy in my class is Beefy Bert.
Once I hit Bert and woke up on the floor,
looking up at the ceiling. He'd better not try
that again.

MOST FANTASTIC FEET...

The largest feet ever recorded belonged to a man from the USA who died in 1940. His feet were over 43 centimetres long – that's longer than two Horrid Henry books laid end to end.

...AND HUGEST HANDS

A Somalian man has the largest hands in the world – they measure nearly 30 cm from his wrists to the tip of his middle fingers – around the length of a comic.

SNEAKIEST SNATCHER

The biggest, fattest, greasiest hands at my school belong to Greasy Greta, the demon dinner lady. She's always snatching the crisps and sweets I bring for my lunch. I got my revenge on her though...

MOST TITANIC TV

The biggest TV ever made is 1.8 metres tall and 3.41 metres wide – that's the same as two double beds pushed together. It's high-definition with a massive plasma screen, and is worth over £300,000.

TEENIEST TINIEST TELLY

My mean parents own the smallest TV in the whole world. It's so miniscule I practically have to watch it using a magnifying glass.

PARTY PIZZA RECORD

The biggest pizza you can buy is 2.37 metres squared – as big as a king-sized duvet and enough to feed 100 people. You can find it at Big Mama's and Papa's Pizzeria in the USA and it costs over £100.

SUPER-SIZE SNACKS

My favourite restaurant, Gobble and Go,
serves the biggest meals in the world – jumbo
burgers, huge pizzas and lakes of ketchup.
I love watching the chefs heat up the food
in their giant microwave.

CHUNKIEST CHOCOLATE

The biggest bar of chocolate ever made weighed 4,410 kg – as heavy as an elephant – and measured 5.69 metres long and 2.79 metres wide – about the size of an Olympic swimming pool. It was created by the Grand Candy Company in the tiny country of Armenia.

I want one - now!

BIGGEST BABY
The biggest baby ever born was a boy weighing 10.8 kg in the USA in 1879. He was three times heavier than most newborn babies!

STUPENDOUS SNOWBALL
It took seven hours to make the largest snowball ever in Austria in 2010. With a circumference of 6.72 metres, this monster snowball would have reached the ceiling of your living room!

LARGEST UNDERPANTS

The largest underpants in the world are 20 metres across the waist and 12 metres from waistband to crotch. That's one seriously big pair of pants.

3. TOP TOYS

BESTSELLING TOY OF ALL TIME

Billions of Barbie dolls have been sold throughout the world since they were launched in 1959. In fact, it's estimated that three Barbie dolls are sold every second.

MY MOST-WANTED TOY OF ALL TIME

Top of my most-wanted list is the Boom-Boom Basher – a toy which crashes and trashes everything in its path, with an ear-piercing siren that wails all the time.

LONGEST COMPUTER GAME

In 1991, a German man played a computer game called *FATE: Gates of Dawn* for 166 hours – nearly a whole week!

TOP COMPUTER TAKEOVER

I got my longest go ever on the computer when Peter was banned for a week for writing a rude essay about his teacher, Miss Lovely (with a little help from me). Ssshh.

MAGNET MADNESS

The largest collection of fridge magnets can be found in Nevada in the USA. It's owned by the Magnet Lady, who has over 30,000 magnets.

FAST FOOD TOY MOUNTAIN

A man from Devon, England, began his collection of McDonald's Happy Meal toys in the 1980s and he now has more than 7,500.

COLOSSAL COLLECTION

A woman from the UK owns the largest collection of Pokémon memorabilia with over 12,000 different items.

GREATEST GIZMO COLLECTION

That worm Peter has ten Gizmos – one of each colour, arranged neatly on his shelf. But I hold the record, with a grand total of 643 – some from Peter's room and the rest from ransacking every Sweet Tweet box in the Happy Shopper supermarket. My collection is arranged in a heap on my bedroom floor and can be viewed for £2.00.

CHAMPION CHEATING

The world's worst cheating was when Moody Margaret played Gotcha with me and Peter. Margaret was the banker and she stole the bank's money. So when I ran out of money, I sneaked round to Margaret's house and pinched all the money from her Gotcha game. Ha ha!

SCRABBLE CHEAT

At the 2012 National Scrabble Championship in Florida, USA, a player was caught hiding two blank letter tiles (blank tiles can be used as any letter, so they help a player to win). He was kicked out of the competition.

MOST EXPENSIVE

The most expensive toy of all time is a steam-powered model of a battleship called HMS Terrible. It was made in 1905, and in 2012 it sold at auction for a massive £90,000.

MY WORST TOY OF ALL TIME

The Walkie-Talkie-Burpy-Slurpy-Teasy-Weasy Doll. The only thing that would be worse than walking around town with this doll would be having to marry Moody Margaret.

WORLD'S WORST PRESENTS

My worst ever collection of Christmas presents was a pen, pencil and ruler, a dictionary, gloves, mints and a pink bow tie from Aunt Ruby. I sent her a five-line No Thank You letter.

4. FOOD GLORIOUS FOOD

DOUGHNUT DEVOURING

The world record for the fastest doughnut eating is held by Ray Meduna from the USA. He can eat 22 doughnuts in 1 minute 39 seconds!

I bet Greedy Graham could eat 23 doughnuts in 1 minute 39 seconds. And I could eat 24 in 1 minute 39 seconds - if only Mum and Dad would buy me that many.

SWEET SPEED-EATING

At my version of the Olympics – the Holympics – I was the champion of the sweet speed-eating competition, with Greedy Graham a close second.

CHOCOLATE-EATING CHAMPION OF THE UNIVERSE!

I chomped my way through 40 giant chocolate bars I bought as prizes for my Holympics when I was practising for the speed-eating contest.

CHOCOLATE CHOMPING CHAMPIONS

The world's chocolate chomping champions are the people of the UK, each eating an average of 12 kg of chocolate per year – that's five small chocolate bars per person every week!

GREEDIEST BOY

Greedy Graham. He always has a bulging bag of toffee, chocolate, lollies and sweets, and a towering stack of chocolate spread sandwiches in his packed lunch.

TOP SNAIL SNACKER

The record for snail-eating is held by Peter Dowdeswell from the UK, who once consumed an entire kilo of snails in garlic (about 80 snails) in 3 minutes 48 seconds.

CHAMPION SAUSAGE SWALLOWER

In 2003, Cecil Walker from the USA swallowed the most sausages ever in one minute – he managed eight without even chewing!

TOP CRISP GUZZLER

I hold the world record for crisp guzzling.
I can scoff an entire pack of Super Spicy
Hedgehog crisps in seventeen seconds,
especially when I'm in class and have to do it
secretly so Miss Battle-Axe doesn't catch me.

SPEEDIEST SPROUTS

Dave Mynard of the UK ate a record 43
Brussels sprouts in one minute in 2003.

SNEAKIEST SECRET

I won the prize for the best way to get out of eating Brussels sprouts. I pretended to eat them while secretly sneaking them into a drawer in the table in front of me. Genius!

CRAZIEST CRACKING

The record for the most eggs cracked in an hour is held by Canadian Bob Blumer who broke open 2,069 eggs with one hand in 2010.

KETCHUP KING

The fastest ketchup drinking record was won by Dustin Phillips from the USA who drank 360 grammes of ketchup through a straw in 33 seconds.

Wow. He must love ketchup even more than I do.

FASTEST FLIPS

The record for the most flips of a pancake in a frying pan is 416 flips in two minutes, held by Ralf Laue of Germany.

MOST MASSIVE MENU

The biggest menu in the world can be found in a restaurant called Mofarguru in Budapest, Hungary – there are 1,810 dishes to choose from.

POSHEST RESTAURANT

The poshest restaurant I've ever been to is Restaurant Le Posh, where I tried snails for the first time.

LARGEST RESTAURANT

The biggest restaurant in the world is the Damascus Gate Restaurant in Syria, with 6,014 seats.

DARKEST RESTAURANT

At Dans Le Noir in London, diners eat
completely in the dark! If you order the
Chef's Surprise, you have to try and guess
what you're eating.

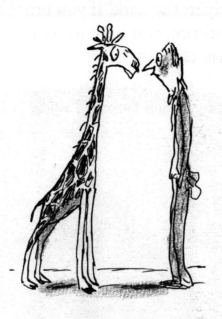

TALLEST PENCIL TOWER

The tallest pencil tower was made from 2,000 pencils and measured 2.9 metres high. It was built by kids at Eisenhower Junior High School in Utah, USA.

DOMINO BALANCING CHAMPION

The largest number of dominoes ever stacked on top of one another is 1,036, by Alexander Bendikov from Belarus.

HORRID HENRY'S TOILET ROLL TOWER

I hold the record for the most toilet rolls ever used in a class Group Project – because I stole everyone else's toilet rolls for my model of the Parthenon.

TALLEST PERSON

Robert Pershing Wadlow from the USA is the tallest known person in the world at 2.72 metres. He died in 1940 but he's still the tallest person ever and he could look into a first floor window of a house without using a ladder.

TALLEST TEACHER

The tallest person in my class is Miss Battle-Axe. And I found out that her mum is even taller, skinnier and scarier when I saw them together at Restaurant Le Posh.

GIANT GEORGE

The tallest known dog in the world is Giant George, a Great Dane from Arizona, USA. George is over one metre tall, the height of an average seven-year old boy, and he sleeps on a full-sized human bed.

TALLEST BUILDING

The tallest skyscraper in the world is in Dubai. It rises 826 metres into the sky and has 160 floors. Inside there are apartments, shops, offices and a restaurant, plus a high-speed lift and a viewing deck on level 124.

SUPER-SIZED SNOWMAN

The tallest snowman in the world was built in Maine, USA, in 1999. Nicknamed Angus, King of the Mountain, he measured 35 metres – as high as a church tower – with two three-metre trees for arms and six car tyres for his mouth.

BIGGEST SNOWMAN BATTLE

When Margaret, Peter and I entered the Frosty Freeze Ice Cream competition to build the biggest snowman, Peter was the winner. His snow bunny was a pathetic little pimple but the other two snowmen melted overnight. Wah!

OLDEST MUMMY

The oldest complete mummy is over 4,500 years old, found in a tomb in Egypt.

MOST STOMACH-CURDLING KIT

Peter's Curse of the Mummy Kit is the grossest, yuckiest, most stomach-curdling kit I've ever seen. It has a plastic body to mummify, mummy-wrapping gauze, and removable mummy organs to put in a jar.

SLIMIEST SNAILS

In 2009, Fin Keleher from the USA broke the world record by having 43 snails on his face all at once for ten seconds at his eleventh birthday party.

Wow. What a great idea.

BIGGEST PANT PARADE

The world record for most people ever gathered together to display their underpants is 116. All these brave people showed their pants to passers-by at St Pancras Station in London in 2008 to raise money for charity.

LONGEST-LASTING TOILET ROLL

The largest roll of toilet paper was created in Peru in 2008. It was 1.7 metres in diameter and had enough paper to last the average human for 100 years.

MOST REVOLTING RHYME

I've got the record for writing the most revolting poem. It's called 'I'm Gonna Throw Up' and it's so repulsive that when I read it out loud, my tough teacher Mr Nerdon turned green.

REPULSIVE RATTLESNAKE RECORD

Jackie Bibby from Texas has been nicknamed The Texas Snake Man. He achieved a world record by having eight rattlesnakes in his mouth at once and another for sitting in the bath with 81 of them!

Maybe I could persuade Stuck-Up Steve to challenge him.

SMELLY FEET

Madeline Albrecht has sniffed the most feet ever – 5,600 over 15 years when she worked for Dr Scholl, a foot care company.

STINKIEST STINKBOMB

Rude Ralph and I made the world's stinkiest stinkbomb with my Stinky Stinkbomb kit. We mixed together Dead Fish powder with Rotten Egg powder. Bleccch!

BEASTLIEST BATH

In 2002, Christine Martin from the UK took the longest ever maggot bath – she sat there for 1 hour 30 minutes.

LICKABLE LIFT

The world's most disgusting lift is in an office block in London. It's decorated with 1,300 Jaffa cake flavoured stickers and people can lick the stickers as they go up and down.

NASTIEST NIBBLES

The most horrible biscuits and chocolate ever can be found at New Nick's house. There are dog hairs all over the sweet jar and teeth marks in the chocolate. Gross!

COW PAT RECORD

The record for throwing a dry cow pat is 81 metres – nearly the length of a football pitch – held by Steve Urner from the USA since 1981.

HORRID HOG HOUSE

Teenagers compete to have the most disgusting bedroom on one of my favourite TV shows, Hog House. I can't wait until I'm a teenager. My bedroom will beat anything on Hog House.

BIGGEST BRUSSELS

The heaviest Brussels sprout ever was grown in Wales in 1992 – it weighed 8.3 kg, more than 8 bags of sugar.

HORRID HENRY'S WORST VEGETABLE

That big Brussels sprout would give me nightmares. Of all the horrible, rotten vegetables ever invented, sprouts are the worst.

MOST FEARSOME FRUIT

The most dangerous apple in the world comes from the Manchineel tree in Florida – just one bite causes severe pain and can even kill.

GRUESOMEST GLOP

Me and Moody Margaret made the most disgusting food ever eaten when we invented Glop. It's a mix of porridge, semolina, coleslaw, spinach, coffee, yoghurt, flour, vinegar, baked beans, mustard, peanut butter, mouldy cheese, pepper, rotten oranges and ketchup.

7. WINNING WORDS

SMALLEST BOOK

The smallest book in the world is the ABC Picture Book by Joshua Reichart. It measures just 2.4 mm x 2.9 mm – around the size of a baby's fingernail, and has 32 pages.

BIGGEST BOOK

The thickest book in the world is 322 mm in width. It was published in London in 2009 and includes all of Agatha Christie's stories about the detective Miss Marple. It has 4,032 pages and costs £1,000.

MAKE-BELIEVE BOOKS

The record for the biggest number of made-up books is held by me. I invented the titles of 22 books in order to win the school reading competition. The first five books on my list really do exist, but I haven't actually read those either – I just copied them from Peter's list!

SPEEDIEST READER

The largest number of library books borrowed in a lifetime is 25,000 – by Louise Brown from Scotland. She has read twelve books a week since 1946.

BORING BOOK WORLD

Book World gets my top prize for being the most boring theme park in the world. Visitors can enjoy a speed-reading display, practise checking out library books, and read to the beat. Aaargh!

CLEVER CLARE

The first girl to learn to read in my class was Clever Clare at two years old. She could also do long division at three, built a telescope at four and compose a symphony at five.

SPELLING BACKWARDS

The record for most words spelled backwards is 14 in a minute, achieved by Emma Britton from the UK in 2011.

SPELLING TEST TERROR

I scored zero in ten spelling tests in a row, which must be a world record for the most rotten spelling ever!

Rinoceros ✗
Daffydil ✗
Crumpit ✗
Garrage ✗
Nessessery ✗
Committy ✗
Handel ✗

TRICKY WORDS

The hardest words in the world to spell (according to me) are: hieroglyphs, trapezium and diarrhoea.

LONGEST WORD

The longest word in the Oxford English Dictionary (not counting the names of some horrible diseases) has 34 letters and means 'wonderful'. It comes from the film of Mary Poppins – it's SUPER-CALI-FRAGI-LISTIC-EXPI-ALI-DOCIOUS.

LONGEST PLACE NAMES

The longest place name in the UK is a town in Wales with 58 letters – LLAN-FAIR-PWLL-GWYN-GYLL-GOGERY-CHWYRN-DROBWLL-LLANTY-SILIO-GOGO-GOCH.

The longest place name in the world has 85 letters! It's a hill in New Zealand called TAUMATA-WHAKA-TANGI-HANGA-KOAUAUO-TAMATEA-TURIPUKAKA-PIKI-MAUNGA-HORO-NUKU-POKAI-WHENUA-KITANA-TAHU.

SHORTEST ALPHABET

Rotokas, a language spoken in Papua New Guinea, has only 12 letters in its entire alphabet – they are A, E, G, I, K, O, P, R, S, T, U and V.

BILLION BESTSELLER

The world's bestselling book of all time is the Holy Bible, with estimated sales of over six billion.

WORST STORY EVER

The World's Worst Story is *The Adventures of Fluff Puff*, written by Peter, all about the adventures of Peter's favourite plastic sheep, Fluff Puff, and the terrible day his pink and yellow nose turned blue.

8. FANTASTIC FACES

LONGEST TONGUE
Stephen Taylor from the UK has the longest tongue in the world. When he sticks it out it measures nearly 10 cm from his lips to the tip of the tongue.

CHEAPEST EVER MAKEOVER
Moody Margaret's Magnificent Makeovers cost only £1. But I topped that by offering a special price of 75p at my Marvellous Makeovers – and I even included free beauty advice. Wonder why it didn't catch on?

LONGEST TOOTH

The longest tooth ever pulled out was 3.2 cm. That's a whole centimetre longer than an average tooth.

MOST BABY TEETH

When Sean Keaney was born on 10th April 1990 in the UK he was an instant world record holder – for already having 12 teeth.

RUDE RALPH'S RECORD

Rude Ralph is in the lead with four lost teeth – two top and two bottom. He can spit to the blackboard from his desk. Wait till I catch up with him.

MOST ENORMOUS EARLOBES

Jian Tianjin, a farmer from Taiwan, has the longest earlobes in the world – they stretch to 16 cm and he can wind them round his chin!

BEARDED LADY

Vivian Wheeler of the USA holds the record for the woman with the longest beard – nearly 28 cm long.

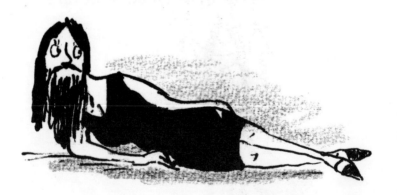

LONGEST EYEBROWS

Leonard Traenkenschuh from Washington, USA, has the world's longest eyebrows with two of the hairs measuring nearly 9 cm. Almost as long as Stephen Taylor's tongue!

MOST MAGNIFICENT MOUSTACHE

The world's longest moustache belongs to Badamsinh Juwansinh Gurjar from India. It measures almost 4 metres.

UGLY SCALE

On Sour Susan's ugly scale – with 1 being the ugliest, wartiest toad, she awarded her best friend, Moody Margaret, a 2. But Margaret gave Susan a minus 1 – she's so ugly she's off the scale.

9. KNOCK-OUT NOISE

LOUDEST SOUND EVER

The loudest ever recorded sound was the eruption of the volcano on the small island of Krakatoa, near Indonesia, in 1883. The sound could be heard from nearly 5,000 km away – roughly the distance from London to New York.

Don't believe this. The loudest ever sound comes from my Root-a-toot trainers.

MOST EAR-SPLITTING SCREAM

Moody Margaret holds the record for the loudest screamer in my class. No one can scream as loud or as long or as piercingly as Moody Margaret.

NOISIEST SLEEPOVER

The noisiest house I ever stayed at was New Nick's. Nick's parents had an opera karaoke club, the radio was on, Nick snored, the winter wind howled through the open window and the dogs barked. It was even too noisy for me!

LONGEST JOKES

The longest joke-telling session was in 1992 when Mike Heeman from the USA told 12,682 jokes over 24 hours.

BOOMING BAND

I am is the world's number one fan of the best and loudest band in the world, the Killer Boy Rats. I've got all their albums – Attack-Tack-Tack, Splat! and Manic Panic, and I love blasting out my favourite Rats song on my Boom-box and singing along at the top of my voice: "I'm dead, you're dead, we're dead."

ATISHOO!

A 12-year old British girl sneezed for the longest recorded time – 977 days from 1981 to 1983. She sneezed every minute for the first year, then every five minutes for the next two years.

HICCUP ATTACK

Charles Osborne from the USA had the longest ever attack of hiccups. He hiccupped for 68 years from 1922 to 1990.

LONGEST COUNTING OUT LOUD

In 2007, Jeremy Harper from the USA counted from one to one million out loud in front of a webcam. It took him 89 days and he raised over £5,000 for charity.

LARGEST WHOOPEE CUSHION

The largest whoopee cushion ever made is three metres in diameter. It was made for a music project in London in 2008.

BIGGEST BURP

The loudest burp ever was 109.9 decibels by Paul Hunn in London in 2009. Talking is about 25-35 decibels, so that burp was almost four times louder!

BEST BURPING
I can burp along to the theme tune of one of my favourite TV presenters, Marvin the Maniac.

10. SCHOOL SUCCESS

HIGHEST SCHOOL

Erping Village Elementary School in China, is built on a platform nearly 3,050 metres above a remote mountainside. Students have to climb wooden ladders to get to their lessons!

BREAKING IN A NEW TEACHER

The quickest time that I've broken in a new teacher is Mrs Zip who left after just one day, breaking my previous record of two weeks, when Miss Marvel ran screaming from the classroom.

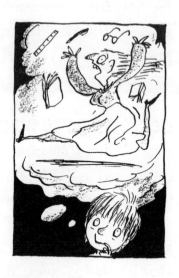

NASTY NERDON

Mr Nerdon holds two records in my school. He's the toughest, meanest, nastiest teacher in the school, and he's the teacher with the most stupid name and nickname – Nerdy Nerd!

CLEVERER THAN CLEVER CLARE

Dr Sainbhy, a super student from India, has a grand total of 35 university degrees. Most people only have one!

GOOD AS GOLD BOOK

Peter holds the school record for entries in the Good as Gold Book with an Outstanding three times in one month.

Huh. If there was a Wormy Worm Book, Peter would win every week.

MOST UNPOPULAR PUDDING

The most hated school dinner food in the UK is tapioca, a milky pudding a bit like rice pudding and nastily nicknamed 'frogspawn'.

MOST DISGUSTING DESSERT

My worst ever school dinner dessert is fruit salad. When I have to eat it, I'm sure I can feel worms slithering in my stomach. Ugggghh!

FAVOURITE FOOD

The most popular school dinner in the UK is fish and chips.

FOOD FIGHT

Students at a school in Utah, USA, set a world record for the largest marshmallow fight by throwing over 140,000 marshmallows in 15 minutes.

TOP TWINS

The world record for the most twins in one year at school is held by Des Moines High School in the USA. There are 32 sets of twins in Ninth Grade (which would be Year 10 in the UK).

OLDEST DANCE TEACHER

The oldest dance teacher in the world is in her nineties. Gisela Weser from Germany was born in 1921 and started teaching dance in 1949.

WORLD'S MOST HORRID DANCE TEACHER

Our dancing teacher, Miss Impatience Tutu, hates teaching and hates children. But most of all, she hates me.

11. TOP TERRORS

POISONOUS SPIDER

The world's most poisonous spider is the Brazilian wandering spider. Its venom is so powerful that the tiniest amount will kill a mouse – and a large amount could kill a fully-grown human.

HORRIBLE AND HAIRY

The most horrible and hairy spider ever seen in my house appeared when Rabid Rebecca was babysitting. I'm not scared of spiders and so I used it to scare Rebecca into letting me watch TV and eat lots of ice cream, sweets, biscuits and crisps.

BIGGEST BIRD-EATING SPIDER

The largest spider in the world is the Goliath bird-eater. It has a leg span of 28 cm and is big enough to cover a dinner plate!

CREEPY-CRAWLIES

The most spiders I've ever seen appeared on Christmas Day when Mum decorated the table with fresh holly and ivy – and millions of spiders ran out and all over the food.

SCARIEST SHARKS

The scariest sharks in the world are Great White Sharks – they have attacked and killed 244 humans to date.

I bet that was a Great White Shark I saw in the swimming pool.

MOST TENTACLED OCTOPUS

In 1998, an amazing octopus was discovered in Japan. Each of its eight tentacles had branched out like a tree – producing a grand total of 96 tentacles.

MOST VENOMOUS SNAKE

The most venomous snake in the world is the Indian Cobra. Its poison takes just a few minutes to kill.

Great. Now I've got the perfect present for Stuck-Up Steve.

TOUGHEST TEEN

Rabid Rebecca holds the record for biggest, meanest, ugliest, nastiest-looking babysitter. Not only did she make Tough Toby do all his homework, she even made Moody Margaret wash the floor!

HIGHEST TIGHTROPE
In 1989 Michael Menin from France performed the highest ever tightrope walk – 3,150 metres above the ground.

TRAPPED
Kively Papajohn from Cyprus was trapped in a lift for six days in 1987 – the longest time on record. Luckily, the 76-year old had just been shopping so she survived on the food she'd bought.

MASSIVE EARTHQUAKE

The largest earthquake ever recorded was in May 1960 in Valdivia, Chile. It caused a tsunami, with local waves that were 25 metres high.

LONGEST NEEDLE

The world record for the longest needle is 980 mm – that's as long as a broom handle! It was given as a present to a doctor when he retired from work, and can be still be seen at a museum in Sheffield in the UK.

No way am I ever looking at that.

NASTIEST NEEDLE

Nurse Needle brings in the Ginormous Needle on Injection Day – it's the longest, sharpest, most wicked needle I've ever seen.

WORST PUNISHMENT

The worst punishment I've ever been threatened with is NO TV for a whole year.

12. SERIOUSLY SILLY

LONGEST NAME

The longest name in the world belonged
to a nineteen-year-old from Somerset, UK,
who changed his name in 2008 to Captain
Fantastic Faster Than Superman Spiderman
Batman Wolverine Hulk And the Flash
Combined. His parents had called him
George.

NASTIEST NICKNAME

My nastiest and longest ever nickname for Peter is Telltale Frogface Ninnyhammer Toady Poo Bag.

ICIEST BATH

Wim Hoff of the Netherlands, nicknamed The Iceman, holds the record for the longest ice bath. In 2011 he stood in a tube filled with ice cubes for 1 hour 52 minutes and 42 seconds. Brrr!

HENRY'S COLDEST BATH

I almost turned into an icicle when I had to share a bath with Peter in freezing water. Peter was sitting at the tap end, which meant he got to control the temperature!

STUFFED WITH STRAWS

In 2009 in Bavaria, Germany, Simon Elmore held 400 straws in his mouth for ten seconds.

HIGHEST FLIPS

The highest a pancake has been tossed and re-caught in a pan is 8.6 metres – that's higher than a house! – by Jean-Marie Livonnen from France.

BIGGEST PIE FIGHT

The largest custard pie fight was in Bolton, UK in 2000 when 3,320 custard pies were thrown in 3 minutes.

SPEEDIEST SOFA

The fastest ever furniture is a sofa called Casual Lofa. Invented in the UK in 1998, it has an engine, leopard skin seat covers, a pizza pan for a steering wheel and it travels at speeds of up to 87 miles per hour.

BEST TIME-TRAVEL TRICK

My Mega-Mean Time Machine trick on Perfect Peter was my greatest trick ever. I tricked Peter into believing that he'd travelled to the future, where boys wear dresses and lipstick, people talk Ugg language and everyone just eats vegetables.

That's a world record for the greatest trick ever played on a little brother or sister.

CHRISTMAS TREE BALANCING CHAMPION

A man from Suffolk balanced a two-metre Christmas tree on his chin during the run up to Christmas in December 2001 for a record breaking time of 56.82 seconds

TOP CHRISTMAS TREE DECORATION

When I replaced the fairy with my Terminator Gladiator toy, it was the strangest ever decoration at the top of a Christmas tree. Our tree also holds the record for the fewest chocolate decorations left on Christmas morning – none at all. I sneaked down in the night and scoffed them all!

CAN BALANCING RECORD

In 2003, John Evans balanced 428 cans of fizzy drink on his head, beating his own previous record of 400 cans!

MOST BALLOONS BLOWN UP
In 2011, Darryl Learie from Canada blew up
446 balloons in one hour on live television

MOST UNDERPANTS
The world record for wearing the most
underpants at the same time is 231, by Taro
Yabe in Japan in 2010.

NASTIEST KNICKERS
I was sent the worst pair of knickers ever
by Great-Aunt Greta for my birthday. They
were frilly pink and lacy, and decorated with
glittery hearts and bows.

PAPERCLIP CHAIN CHAMPION
In 2004, the longest paperclip chain was made in 24 hours by Dan Meyer from the USA. He used over 54,000 paperclips to create a 1,629 metre-long chain.

OLDEST MESSAGE IN A BOTTLE
The oldest message in a bottle was found by a fisherman in Shetland after 92 years and 229 days at sea.

LAST POST
A postcard bringing holiday news to a couple in West Yorkshire, England, was delivered in 2009 – 40 years after it was posted.

HORRID HENRY BOOKS

Horrid Henry
Horrid Henry and the Secret Club
Horrid Henry Tricks the Tooth Fairy
Horrid Henry's Nits
Horrid Henry Gets Rich Quick
Horrid Henry's Haunted House
Horrid Henry and the Mummy's Curse
Horrid Henry's Revenge
Horrid Henry and the Bogey Babysitter
Horrid Henry's Stinkbomb
Horrid Henry's Underpants
Horrid Henry Meets the Queen
Horrid Henry and the Mega-Mean Time Machine
Horrid Henry and the Football Fiend
Horrid Henry's Christmas Cracker
Horrid Henry's Christmas Cracker
Horrid Henry and the Abominable Snowman
Horrid Henry Robs the Bank
Horrid Henry Wakes the Dead
Horrid Henry Rocks
Horrid Henry and the Zombie Vampire
Horrid Henry's Monster Movie
Horrid Henry's Nightmare

Early Readers

Colour Books

Joke Books

Horrid Henry's Joke Book
Horrid Henry's Jolly Joke Book
Horrid Henry's Might Joke Book
Horrid Henry versus Moody Margaret
Horrid Henry's Hilariously Horrid Joke Book
Horrid Henry's Purple Hand Gang Joke Book
Horrid Henry's All Time Favourite Joke Book

Activity Books

Horrid Henry's Brainbusters
Horrid Henry's Headscratchers
Horrid Henry's Mindbenders
Horrid Henry's Colouring Book
Horrid Henry's Puzzle Book
Horrid Henry's Sticker Book
Horrid Henry's Classroom Chaos
Horrid Henry's Holiday Havoc
Horrid Henry Runs Riot
Horrid Henry's Annual 2014

Visit **Horrid Henry**'s website at www.horridhenry.co.uk for competitions, games, downloads and a monthly newsletter.

the orion star

Sign up for **the orion star** newsletter to get inside information about your favourite children's authors as well as exclusive competitions and early reading copy giveaways.

www.orionbooks.co.uk/newsletters

Follow @the_orionstar on .